Radical Sports

CAVING

Chris Howes • • • • • • • • • • • • •

Heinemann Library
Chicago, Illinois

© 2003 Reed Educational & Professional Publishing
Published by Heinemann Library,
an imprint of Reed Educational & Professional Publishing,
Chicago, Illinois

Customer Service 888-454-2279
Visit our website at www.heinemannlibrary.com

Designed by Celia Floyd
Illustrations by Jeff Edwards (p. 18) and Rhian Hicks (p. 23)
Originated by Universal
Printed in Hong Kong

07 06 05 04 03
10 9 8 7 6 5 4 3 2 1

Library of Congress Cataloging-in-Publication Data

Howes, Chris, 1951-
  Caving / Chris Howes.
      p. cm. -- (Radical sports)
Includes bibliographical references and index.
Summary: A beginner's guide to caving, with a brief history of the sport
and information on supplies and equipment, basic safety, techniques,
training, working as a team, and finding caves to explore.
  ISBN 1-58810-626-8 25.64
  1. Caving--Juvenile literature. [1. Caving. 2. Caves.] 1. Title. II.
Series.
  GV200.62 .H69 2002
  796.52'5--dc21

                              2001004801

Acknowledgments

The author and publishers are grateful to the following for permission to reproduce copyright material:
All photographs Chris Howes/Wild Places Photography, except Stockfile, p. 12 (upper).

Cover photograph reproduced with permission of Chris Howes/Wild Places Photography.

Our thanks to Caving Supplies of Buxton, U.K., for loan of equipment, and to Jane Bingham and Hazel Barton for their comments in the preparation of this book.

Every effort has been made to contact copyright holders of any material reproduced in this book. Any omissions will be rectified in subsequent printings if notice is given to the publisher.

Some words are shown in bold, **like this.** You can find out what they mean by looking in the glossary.

Never enter a cave on your own or without having gained suitable experience.

CONTENTS

INTRODUCTION

Caves are fascinating places that invite all sorts of questions. Where does the dark passage lead? How deep is that hole and can we reach the bottom? Where does the water go?

Caving allows you to explore gigantic **chambers** with impressive waterfalls and amazing mineral **formations,** and there is always the chance that you might discover a place where no one has ever been. Caving combines skills such as climbing, swimming, and map reading, but you don't have to be super-fit to take part. That's because there are different grades of caves—some are difficult to descend and some are easy.

This well-equipped caver is placing his feet carefully as he follows the water in a **streamway.**

DIFFERENT NAMES

- **Caver** someone who explores caves

- **Potholer** caver who explores **potholes** (caves with a vertical entrance)

- **Speleologist** someone who explores and studies caves for science

- **Spelunker** untrained and poorly equipped person who has entered a cave for sport

A short history

For centuries, caves have attracted people wanting to satisfy their curiosity. **Archaeologists** have uncovered animal bones and the remains of prehistoric people in caves. Tourists have marveled at the wonders that lie beneath the earth.

No one person can be said to have "invented" caving. However, in 1888, Édouard Martel of France began exploring caves for sport as well as for study. He visited England in 1895 and, using a rope ladder, descended the vast 360 feet (110 meters) deep shaft of Gaping Gill in Yorkshire, succeeding where others had failed. This exciting feat triggered a new interest in exploring caves, and caving as a sport spread around the world.

This drawing is of Édouard Martel using a rope ladder to descend the vast entrance shaft of Gaping Gill in 1895.

Caving today

Caves are found in virtually every country of the world. Many are easy to find near roads or even in towns, but some lie high on mountains or deep in jungles. Others are hidden so well that no one has found them yet. Thousands of people take part in caving, simply because exploring caves is exciting and fun!

Getting Started

Caving is a very safe sport when approached with care. Modern cavers use specialized clothing and equipment to make exploring caves safer, but there are also rules that must be followed. One of the most basic rules is that you must never enter a cave on your own—if you have even a minor accident, such as a twisted ankle, you will need help.

Everyone can go caving—it is a sport for all ages and sizes. You don't have to be small and thin to be a caver. However, you will need training before you can go caving. You will learn some things underground, but a lot of training will take place on the surface.

Where can I learn?

You may have already visited a **showcave** while you were on vacation; you can find the closest one to your home by contacting the National Caves Association. A showcave is a cave that is open to tourists, with paths and electric lights, but passages usually extend well beyond the public area. Many showcaves offer "wild" tours so that beginners can go caving with an experienced guide.

You will need training before you descend a cave on a rope.

Top Tip

- Caving is not a competition where you have to be the fastest person and beat your friends to the finish line. Move at your own pace while underground. You are there to discover a new world, not to race to the other end of the cave.

The guide will provide the equipment you need, such as a helmet, kneepads, and light. If you want to learn more, ask the guide after the tour. There is a good chance that he or she will be a caver and can put you in touch with the right people.

There are caving clubs, called grottos. They mostly belong to the National Speleological Society, which produces a "getting started" pamphlet. It has a special section to encourage younger cavers. Its annual convention is ideal for meeting cavers and learning more about the sport. The society can put you in contact with your nearest grotto.

Caves are formed by water, so experienced cavers expect to find streams and waterfalls.

Teamwork

Teamwork is very important in caving, so groups of between four and six cavers usually work together. This means that there are enough people to help others through difficult sections of the cave and to carry equipment that will be used by everyone.

YOUR PERSONAL EQUIPMENT

Your choice of clothing will depend on the type of cave you are exploring. Some caves are drafty and wet with water flowing through them, while others can be dry and dusty. Although caves stay about the same temperature year-round, this can be cold or warm depending on where you are in the world. Take the advice of an experienced caver when you prepare for your caving expedition.

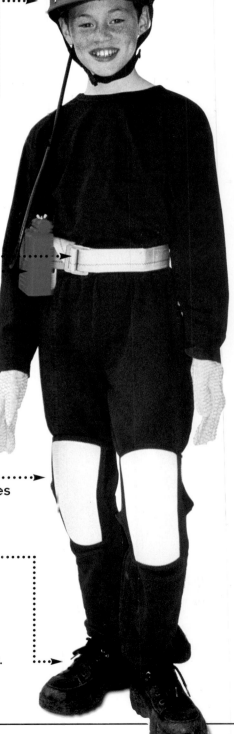

Light

Helmet
Your helmet will protect you if you fall or hit your head on the roof of a passage. It will also protect your head from falling rocks.

Belt

Battery for light

Old clothes
Old clothes are good for easy, dry caves.

Gloves
Gloves can help to protect your hands from getting scratched. You should always wear gloves in an unfamiliar cave.

Kneepads
Good kneepads are essential to protect you when you crawl over rocks. Make sure you have the right size: too tight prevents easy movement and too loose slides down your leg. Sometimes cavers also wear elbow pads.

Boots
The best boots for caving are hiking boots made from synthetic material with good ankle support and soles that grip well. Running shoes are unsuitable and leather boots become stiff after caving in water. Quick-lace hooks are dangerous because they can catch on ladders and ropes. Wear thick, comfortable socks.

The best choice of clothes for easy, **dry caves** is usually something old that you don't mind getting muddy, wet, or torn. Outer clothing should be loose-fitting to allow freedom of movement—a one-piece coverall is a good choice. Do not wear jeans as these will be tight, cold, and clammy when wet.

Helmet

A high-quality caving helmet is vital. Make sure that the helmet is comfortable and does not fall over your eyes when you move—the cradle inside is adjustable. Only use a helmet designed specifically for caving; never use an industrial "hard hat." It will not fully protect you in a fall.

Safety standard mark

Caving helmets and other specialized equipment will carry a UIAA or CE sticker or badge showing that they meet international standards.

Lights

There are several types of caving lights, all of which clip onto the helmet so that you can keep both hands free. Rechargeable batteries are carried on the back of the helmet or on a belt, and can power the latest **LED lights** for many hours. Some lights produce a beam while others, like LED lights, give a very even light. Try caving with different types before you decide which one to buy.

EXTRA EQUIPMENT

Cavers wear special clothing in caves that are cold or wet. Protective oversuits and undersuits help to keep cavers warm, even if they have been in water. However, if you have to be in wet conditions for a long time, a wetsuit is the best choice of clothing.

Undersuit

This well-equipped caver is wearing a one-piece undersuit manufactured from a stretchy fleece-like material. Water drains quickly and the fleece remains warm even when wet.

Oversuit

Oversuits are tough, waterproof, and have a built-in hood that folds away when not in use. Most heat is lost through the head, so wear the hood underneath your helmet in cold caves. Oversuits are made in one piece to keep water out and avoid catching on rocks.

Harness

A caving harness is used to attach a **safety rope** when making climbs and for **SRT.**

Cave pack

A cave pack is used to carry gear such as ladders, ropes, climbing equipment, and a first aid kit that will be used by the team.

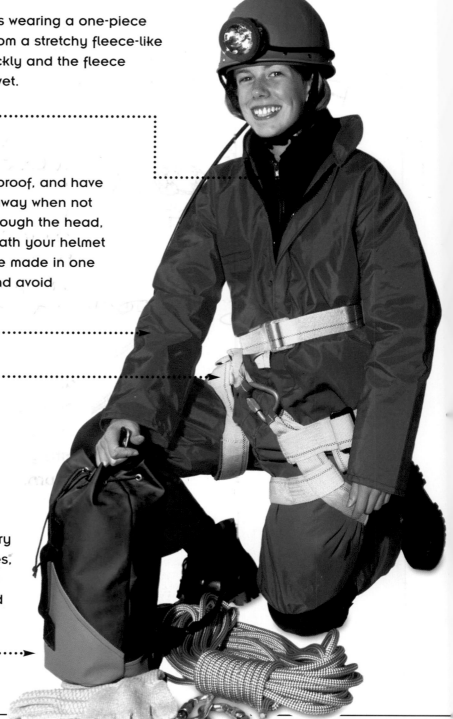

This caver is in very wet conditions and is wearing a wetsuit.

Wetsuit

Wetsuits are made of a rubber called **neoprene** that helps you to float and keeps you warm. A wetsuit should fit snugly; water will still creep in, but it soon warms up next to your skin.

Carrying your gear

As well as ropes and other team equipment, cavers carry water, food, a spare light (or two!), plus extra batteries and bulbs. Cavers may add these things to the team's equipment to avoid having many separate packs. Or, they may carry these things in a smaller, personal cave pack. Caving packs are smooth and do not have many straps, so there are fewer parts to catch on rocks. Because you are part of a team, you may end up carrying your friends' equipment and they will help with yours—everyone takes a turn.

Wearing the correct gear, an undersuit and waterproof oversuit, will help when tackling demanding situations.

Checks and Preparations

Keeping fit

You are not in a race while you are underground, so there is nothing to stop you from resting if you need to. However, you will need stamina—the ability to keep going for a long time, perhaps for many hours. You will also need to be flexible in order to fit through narrow **squeezes.**

The right food

You should eat a healthy diet to stay fit. How much energy you have depends on the types of food you eat. When you are exercising, eat energy-rich meals that are high in **carbohydrates** such as cereals or oatmeal, pasta, rice, and potatoes.

Get plenty of exercise between caving trips. Jogging, cycling, and swimming are all sports that help build stamina and flexibility.

······· *Taking food underground*

Some trips underground will last for several hours, so you will need to take food and drink with you. Avoid carrying heavy, bulky food, since you may have to travel through very narrow passages. Do not be tempted to take only chocolate and junk food. Although these provide a quick burst of energy, their effects soon wear off. Good choices are dried fruit, such as apricots, or energy bars.

Take plenty of liquid to drink, as it is important not to become **dehydrated.** Carry drinks in a plastic bottle (never glass, it might break in a squeeze), or buy small drink cartons with a straw attached. These can be squashed flat afterwards so they are smaller to carry out.

A sheet of plastic or aluminum foil is useful—spread it out while you are eating to catch crumbs. You should never leave any trace of where you have been. Even small particles of food can upset the delicate balance of life found in caves.

Checking the weather

Some caves are unsafe to visit during questionable weather. Rain that has fallen a week before can unexpectedly cause a cave to flood. If it has been raining, or if rain is forecast, you should put off your trip until another day or explore a drier cave.

Staying in touch

Always tell somebody where you have gone and how long you will be. Remember to call when you are out of the cave so that everyone knows that the team is safe. Don't forget to bring money for the phone.

SAFETY FIRST

🦇 When you prepare for your trip, be sure that your gear is in good condition—you will rely on it while underground. Take care of your equipment—repair any tears in clothing, recharge your batteries, and check that your light works properly. Make sure spares, such as batteries and bulbs, are also in good condition.

MOViNG UNDERGROUND

Cave entrances can be horizontal or vertical (vertical entrances are sometimes called **potholes**). Never approach a vertical entrance without being tied to a rope, as it may be unfenced with a sloping or slippery edge.

These two cave entrances are very different. A caver is forced to squeeze into the entrance above, but the entrance below is easily large enough to walk into.

The underground experience

Cave passages twist, turn, and change shape from small and narrow to tall and wide. So, you need to use different techniques to travel through them. Most people think of caves as always being tight and uncomfortable, but this is far from true as they may contain huge **chambers** or caverns.

SAFETY UNDERGROUND

🦇   Never attempt anything that you are unsure about. You might be nervous the first time you try to pass a **squeeze.** Don't be afraid to ask for help.

🦇   Keep thinking: don't just follow the person in front.

Crawling and squeezing

However large the passage is, sooner or later you will find a place where it gets narrow or boulders block the way. You will have to crawl or squeeze through a small space to where the passage becomes larger again.

When a passage is particularly low, you have to lie down and wriggle—cavers call this a belly-crawl.

Before you enter a small hole in a cave, look to see whether it twists and heads uphill or downhill. If the hole goes downhill, it is easier and safer to enter it feet first.

A good collapse

If there are many fallen rocks in a heap that fills the passage this may be part of a **boulder collapse.** You might think that boulders can fall anywhere at any time in a cave, but this is unlikely. Caves have been there for millions of years and are very stable. However, always be careful in a boulder collapse in case any rocks are loose. They might not fall on you, but they can still wobble and roll.

TOP TIP

Passage floors are rarely flat. Sometimes passages are clean and washed by water, but others may be covered in sand, mud, or boulders. You must watch where you place every footstep to avoid slipping on mud or tripping over a loose rock. Even a minor fall underground can be serious.

Traversing

Sometimes cavers want to avoid traveling along the
floor of a passage because it is full of water
or covered in boulders. If the passage is the right shape
and size, cavers can use a technique called **traversing.**

Coping with water

Sooner or later you will get very
wet when following the path the water
takes as it flows down a passage.
Sometimes cavers have to cross deep
pools, so be sure to tell someone if
you cannot swim.

When a passage roof lowers until
it almost meets a water surface, this
forms a **duckunder**—a place where
there is hardly any air space and you
have to duck through to the other side.
Do not underestimate how cold the
water can be, even if you are wearing
a wetsuit. Cavers often lie on their back
to go through a duckunder so that they
can keep their noses in the air.

To traverse in c passage with good
footholds, place one foot and one
hand on either wall and "walk" along
the passage, legs astride. In narrower
passages put your back on one wall
and both feet on the other.

SAFETY FIRST

* Only enter the water when and
  where an experienced caver
  tells you it is safe.

* Never enter a duckunder
  without supervision.

* Leave **sumps** to the cave diver!

This caver is in a duckunder. Because he planned ahead, he knew he would need to wear a wetsuit.

A sump forms where the passage is totally filled with water. This is the domain of the cave diver, a very specialized type of caver. Even tackling a duckunder requires great care and only the most experienced cavers take up cave diving.

GRADING CAVES

- Although there is always the chance to discover a totally new part of a cave, most passages have already been explored. The best route to take and what equipment is needed will be known by local cavers. Some regions may have guidebooks that detail the location and nature of the caves.

- Caves are graded according to difficulty. There is no international scale of grades but, in general, a low number indicates an easy cave and a high number represents a difficult one. Grades can only be a rough guide to difficulty. What a tall person finds easy, a short one will not and vice versa.

Grade 1	Easy	No **pits** or difficulties
Grade 2	Moderate	May include small climbs or pits
Grade 3	Difficult	Some sections require stamina, but there are no particular hazards
Grade 4	More Difficult	Hazardous sections present, such as large pits or long **crawlways**
Grade 5	Severe	Very strenuous with mixed hazards such as wet pits; rescue may be difficult or impossible

USING A SAFETY ROPE

A **safety rope** is used for protection when on a climb so that you are supported and cannot hit the ground if you fall. The rope used in climbing will stretch a little if this happens. This means that it absorbs the force of the fall without hurting the caver.

Tying the knot

Before cavers can use a safety rope, they must attach it to themselves. To do this, a figure eight knot is tied at the end of the rope.

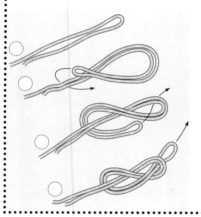

Practice tying a figure eight knot until you can do it perfectly, even in total darkness. Add an overhand knot to ensure it cannot come undone.

figure eight knot

overhand knot

locking karabiner

snapgate karabiner

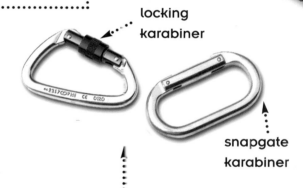

Clipping in

The safety rope is attached to the caver's harness, which may be carried in the **cave pack** until needed. The harness is worn around the waist and legs. The figure eight knot is attached to the front of the harness using a **karabiner.** This is called clipping in. There are different types of karabiners. For caving, always use a locking karabiner and close it securely so that it cannot open by mistake.

Belaying

The other end of the rope is held by another caver who is called the **belayer.** The rest of the team takes turns to make the climb, while the belayer holds the rope. The belayer is protected from falling by using a rope that attaches to an **anchor** point on the cave wall. This could be a handy rock or a hole that the rope can be threaded through. For safety, two or three anchors are used together in case one comes loose. The belayer feeds the rope in or out as required by the climbing caver, so that there is no slack in the rope and the caver cannot fall more than a few inches.

This caver is using a rope to descend a **pit.**

Caring for your rope

Lives depend on the quality of the safety rope. Never stand on a rope—this can force dirt and mud into it, which might cause damage and weaken it. Clean ropes thoroughly after each use and hang them up to dry.

SAFETY FIRST

🦇 Have your harness and knots checked by an experienced caver until you are sure you have everything correct. With practice, it will become second nature to prepare and clip onto the rope.

GOING VERTICAL

A cave passage can suddenly turn into a vertical drop or **pit** that you have to find a way down. Of course, coming in the other direction, you have to climb up in order to move forward. The techniques involved are called descending and ascending.

Ladder and line

For short pits, cavers sometimes use a flexible ladder made from wire cables and metal rungs. Wire ladders are normally about 25 feet (7 meters) long, but they can be linked together for longer drops. Practice climbing up and down a ladder before you go underground. Support your weight on your legs, not your arms, and climb using both hands and one foot behind the ladder, hooking in with your heel. This helps to keep you upright. A **safety rope** is attached to your harness to prevent you from falling while you use the ladder.

Single Rope Technique

On long pits, cavers use the Single Rope Technique **(SRT).** This technique uses a single rope, which cavers climb up using **ascenders** or slide down using **descenders.**

An SRT rope is very different from a safety rope. During SRT, the caver travels along the rope, so it has to withstand a lot of rubbing.

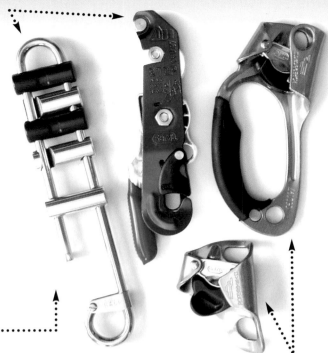

descenders

To climb up an SRT rope, cavers use two ascenders. These slide upward along the rope but then grip it so they cannot slide back down. By alternately putting weight on one ascender while the other is moved up, a caver can climb in safety.

To descend, or **rappel,** cavers are attached to the rope using a single descender. This grips the rope but allows it to slide under the caver's control, so that you slowly descend.

ascenders

For safety reasons, a safety rope needs to stretch a little when a caver falls while attached to it. But if an SRT rope stretched, the caver would bounce up and down while ascending. To avoid bouncing, SRT ropes are very tough and hardly stretch at all.

Practice SRT on the surface before trying it underground. SRT is extremely safe and great fun when the technique is carried out correctly, but you should only try it with an experienced caver.

SRT SAFETY

- Use a locking **karabiner** and be sure it is locked.

- Use the right type of rope; never use a safety rope as an SRT rope or an SRT rope as a safety rope.

- Experienced cavers have died by being careless. Don't be one of them—check all your equipment before you start.

- Train, train, and train some more—then enjoy yourself!

FiNDiNG YOUR WAY

Reading the cave

You should always know where you are in a cave. Sometimes a passage looks the same in both directions—especially after you have taken a break and forgotten which way you came in. Since some areas of a cave may be like a maze, how do you know which way is out? Cavers do not leave trails of paper or unravel balls of string to follow; they take note of their surroundings and know where they are at all times. Everyone has to know the way out in case someone else on the team has an accident.

Use natural features to help, such as whether you are traveling downhill or uphill. Are you moving with or against the flow of water? As you pass an intersection, turn and look back: remember what it looks like because this is what you will see when you return.

Cave **formations** such as **stalactites** or **stalagmites** form landmarks that will help you to remember the way.

Mapping the cave

Cavers make maps, or surveys, of caves to help with planning the trip. Maps indicate hazards and are useful for finding a route. A good map will give clues that cavers use to help them find new passages.

There are many types of cave maps. The most basic ones are sketched from memory. You can do this yourself after your first trip. Others are more accurately drawn, produced after a cave has been measured using a compass and measuring tape.

A cave map

Maps have symbols to show some of the obstacles. Cavers use the information to plan a route and figure out what equipment they may need.

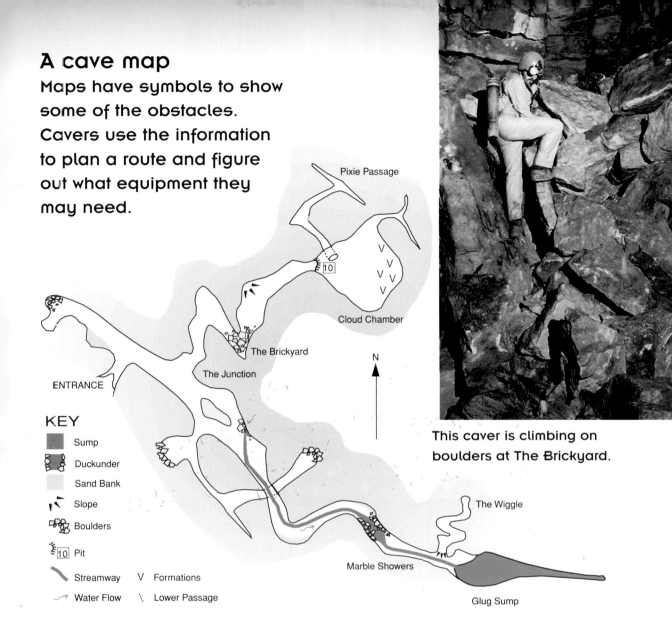

Pixie Passage

Cloud Chamber

The Brickyard

The Junction

ENTRANCE

N

This caver is climbing on boulders at The Brickyard.

The Wiggle

Marble Showers

Glug Sump

KEY

- ▨ Sump
- ▨ Duckunder
- ░ Sand Bank
- ⌁ Slope
- ⌁ Boulders
- 10 Pit
- ⌁ Streamway
- ⌁ Water Flow
- V Formations
- ⋱ Lower Passage

Imagine you are going into this cave. From The Junction you have two choices: follow the water or go through a **boulder collapse** at The Brickyard. Following the water means that you will need a wetsuit to pass through the **duckunder** and your trip ends at a **sump.** You need an **SRT** kit to pass the **pit** on the other route, but you can reach Cloud Chamber, which is filled with formations.

Careful planning and experience allows this caver to pass through the duckunder at Marble Showers.

SAFETY UNDERGROUND

Working together

Caving is a team sport—you help others and they help you. The team should move at the speed of its slowest member. That might be a different person in different situations, so always make sure that the caver behind you is not falling behind. Do not force anyone to move faster than they are comfortable with, and slow down if you feel you are moving too fast for safety. Make sure you never separate from the group and always follow the most experienced caver's advice.

A tired caver is more likely to have an accident, so take even more care near the end of a trip. If you are tired, then tell someone. Eating energy food or taking a break might be the answer. Watch for anyone else who appears tired. Always be prepared to turn back before you have reached where you intended to go. It might be a long way back to the surface.

These cavers are working together by using a raft to safely cross deep water in a French cave.

If things go wrong

Every sport has things that can go wrong, but in caving even a minor problem can quickly become a major one. Teams should carry a basic first aid kit and everyone must know how to use it. Attending a first aid course is a good idea.

Other emergencies can occur. After heavy rain or when snow is melting, some caves can completely fill with water, though it is more likely that only a short section of passage will fill up. This can temporarily trap an unknowing party beyond a **sump.** If you have planned your trip properly, this should not happen to you. If it does, you will have to wait until the passage drains once more. If you are trapped in a cave, you should do everything you can to help yourself, like staying warm and dry.

Take extra care when traveling through fast-flowing water.

If a member of your team is severely injured, at least two cavers should go to the surface to get help. If a team is lost or delayed, others will realize when you do not return on time and get help.

SAFETY FIRST

- 🦇 Take breaks when you need them.
- 🦇 Take the appropriate food.
- 🦇 Tell your team leader if you are cold or tired.

YOU AND THE CAVE

So you've been caving and you want to progress. You will improve your skills simply by going caving and getting experience—especially with techniques such as **SRT.** There is probably a grotto nearby, where cavers can discuss the latest gear and where to find the best caves.

All caving trips have a purpose. Often, this is to learn more about the cave and how it formed. There are always questions to be answered, such as where the water flows to after it has disappeared into a **sump** or where the best place is to look for new passages.

Cavers develop specialties within the sport and study some aspect of caving that fascinates them. Almost any interest you have can be applied to caving, from biology to photography. Learning more about the underground world is an important and fascinating part of caving.

Formations are delicate: look but never touch!

Conserving the cave

Caves are not playgrounds; they are formed by nature and are "non-renewable." That is, we cannot make more caves if we damage the ones we have. Do your part to keep the cave as it is now: never litter, and watch where you place every footstep. Some areas with formations or untouched mud floors may be protected by **flagging tape** that serves as a warning not to get too close. Touching formations such as **stalactites** and **stalagmites** can damage them, because oil from your skin stops the formation from growing.

Paths may be lined with flagging tape. Do not cross it for any reason.

Never leave any sign that you have been in the cave. It should remain the same for the next team to discover and explore.

Bats

Some types of bats live in caves. These animals will not harm you, but they may die if they are disturbed, so never approach or handle a bat. To ensure that bats are given a safe place to live, some caves have a gate across the entrance that keeps people out but allows bats to fly through.

YOUR RESPONSIBILITY

- Take nothing but pictures; do not even leave footprints.

- Respect the cave and the animals that live in it.

- Carry out everything you brought in.

Caves are found in nearly every country of the world—wherever there is **limestone,** there are caves. Because one of the driving forces of caving is exploration, expeditions regularly set out to discover new caves in uncharted regions. This makes caving a truly international sport with literally hundreds of thousands of caves to visit.

Wonderful **formations** decorate this **chamber** in Carlsbad Caverns.

North America

Cavers in the United States have a multitude of caves to seek out. The area bounded by Tennessee, Alabama, and Georgia is known as TAG Country (after the initials of the states). This area offers a lot of options for **SRT.** Some national parks are based on caves, like Mammoth Cave in Kentucky and New Mexico's Carlsbad Caverns.

A caver (circled) shows the huge size of this entrance at Jenolan.

Australasia

One of the most important caving regions in Australia is Tasmania, which is famous for its deep cave systems. The mountains near Sydney hold classic caving areas such as Jenolan and Bungonia. The flat plains of the Nullarbor contain long, shallow, flooded caves that are explored by divers. Over 7,000 caves have been discovered in Australia. New Zealand has two major caving regions—Waitomo on North Island and Nelson on South Island.

Asia

In Sarawak, on the island of Borneo, Gunung Mulu National Park is famous for Sarawak Chamber. Discovered in 1981 by British cavers, it is the world's largest known chamber at 2000 feet (600 meters) long and 1400 feet (415 meters) wide. That's three times the size of the Superdome in New Orleans.

Europe

Europe has a wide range of caves, including most of the world's deepest caves, as well as caves high on mountains that contain permanent ice formations. In France, caving is considered a major sport. The Gouffre Berger is a deep cave that is visited each year by international expeditions.

The major cave regions of the British Isles lie in the Yorkshire Dales, the Peak District, South Wales, the Mendip Hills, and in parts of Ireland.

Into the record book

The longest known cave in the world is Mammoth Cave in Kentucky. It is 330 miles (530 kilometers) long. In January 2001, Krubera—a cave in the Caucasus Mountains of Georgia in Central Asia—became the world's deepest known cave when explorers descended more than a mile (1710 meters) below the surface.

These formations are in a cave in South Wales that was discovered in 1994. More than 40 miles (64 kilometers) of passage have already been explored.

GLOSSARY

anchor attachment point for a rope, often a bolt or suitably shaped rock; also known as a belay point

archaeologist person who studies the remains of past human lives and activities

ascender device attached to an SRT rope that slides upward and grips the rope

belaying technique of holding a rope to protect a climber from falling

boulder collapse section of cave filled with fallen boulders

carbohydrate food that the body uses for energy

caving pack bag used to carry equipment

chamber part of a cave that is larger than the passages leading to and from it

collapse section of cave filled with fallen boulders

crawlway low section of cave that forces you to crawl on your hands and knees

dehydrated condition when you have less water in your body than you should

descender device attached to a rope that allows a caver to slide downward under control

dry cave cave without flowing water, though it may still be wet and muddy with occasional pools

duckunder passage where water nearly touches the roof, only leaving a small air space

flagging tape plastic tape used to mark areas that cavers should not enter

formation general term for stalactites, stalagmites, and similar deposits that grow in caves

karabiner strong metal clip used to attach a rope to an anchor or harness

LED light light made with light-emitting diodes, which lasts for many hours on one set of batteries

limestone rock in which most caves are formed

neoprene rubber material used to make wetsuits, gloves, and socks

pit vertical drop requiring equipment to climb up or down it

pothole cave with a vertical entrance

rappel technique used to slide safely down a rope using friction to slow the descent

safety rope rope used by a caver or climber to keep from falling

showcave cave visited by tourists, usually with concrete floors and electric lights

squeeze small or tight section of cave

SRT Single Rope Technique, used for ascending or descending a vertical drop

stalactite cave formation growing downward from the ceiling

stalagmite cave formation growing upward from the floor

streamway cave passage with a flowing stream or river

sump flooded section of a cave with no air space

traverse horizontal move across a vertical drop, perhaps along a ledge

wet cave cave that contains flowing water, such as a stream or river

USEFUL ADDRESSES

American Cave Conservation
Association
119 East Main Street
P.O. Box 409
Horse Cave, KY 42749

National Caves Association
P.O. Box 280
Park City, KY 42160

National Speleological Society
2813 Cave Avenue
Huntsville, AL 35810-4431

MORE BOOKS TO READ

Brimner, Larry Dane. *Caving: Exploring Limestone Caves.* Danbury, Conn.:
    Franklin Watts, 2001.

Champion, Neil. *Rock Climbing.* Chicago: Heinemann Library, 1999.

Gallant, Roy A. *Limestone Caves.* Danbury, Conn.: Franklin Watts, 1998.

INDEX